THE HUMAN AURA

ASTRAL COLORS AND THOUGHT FORMS

THE HUMAN AURA

ASTRAL COLORS AND THOUGHT FORMS

WILLIAM WALKER ATKINSON

AN ATKINSON BOOK

AN ATKINSON BOOK

Published by White Ivy Press.

CONTENTS

INTRODUCTION: Who Was William Walker Atkinson?
by Karl Wurf 7

CHAPTER I: WHAT IS THE HUMAN AURA? 11

CHAPTER II: THE PRANA-AURA 15

CHAPTER III: THE ASTRAL COLORS 19

CHAPTER IV: THE ASTRAL COLORS (Continued) 23

CHAPTER V : THE AURIC KALEIDOSCOPE 27

CHAPTER VI: THOUGHT FORMS 31

CHAPTER VII : PSYCHIC INFLUENCE OF COLORS 35

CHAPTER VIII: AURIC MAGNETISM 39

CHAPTER IX : DEVELOPING THE AURA 43

CHAPTER X: THE PROTECTIVE AURA 47

INTRODUCTION: WHO WAS WILLIAM WALKER ATKINSON?

BY KARL WURF

William Walker Atkinson (December 5, 1862 – November 22, 1932) was an attorney, merchant, publisher, and author, as well as an occultist and an American pioneer of the New Thought movement. He is also known to have been the author of the pseudonymous works attributed to Theron Q. Dumont and Yogi Ramacharaka.

Due in part to Atkinson's intense personal secrecy and extensive use of pseudonyms, he is now largely forgotten, despite having written more than 100 books in the last 30 years of his life. (He obtained mention in past editions of *Who's Who in America*, *Religious Leaders of America*, and several similar publications—but these are mostly subscription based, and reflect more on his desire to be known than his contemporary fame.) His works have remained in print more or less continuously since 1900.

* * * *

William Walker Atkinson was born in Baltimore, Maryland on December 5, 1862, to William and Emma Atkinson. He began his working life as a grocer at 15 years old, probably helping his father. He married Margret Foster Black of Beverly, New Jersey, in October 1889, and they had two children. The first probably died young. The second later married and had two daughters.

Atkinson pursued a business career from 1882 onwards, and in 1894 he was admitted as an attorney to the Bar of Pennsylvania. While he gained much material success in his profession as a lawyer, the stress and over-strain eventually took its toll, and during this time he experienced a complete physical and mental breakdown, and financial disaster. He looked for healing, and in the late 1880s he found it with New Thought, later attributing the restoration of his health, mental vigor, and material prosperity to the application of the principles of New Thought.

Some time after his healing, Atkinson began to write articles on the truths he felt he had discovered, which were then known as Mental

Science. In 1889, an article by him entitled "A Mental Science Catechism" appeared in Charles Fillmore's new periodical, *Modern Thought*.

By the early 1890s, Chicago had become a major center for New Thought, mainly through the work of Emma Curtis Hopkins, and Atkinson decided to move there. Once in the city, he became an active promoter of the movement as an editor and author. He was responsible for publishing the magazines *Suggestion* (1900–1901), *New Thought* (1901–1905) and *Advanced Thought* (1906–1916).

In 1900, Atkinson worked as an associate editor of *Suggestion, a New Thought Journal*, and wrote his probable first book, *Thought-Force in Business and Everyday Life*, being a series of lessons in personal magnetism, psychic influence, thought-force, concentration, will-power, and practical mental science.

He then met Sydney Flower, a well-known New Thought publisher and businessman, and teamed up with him. In December, 1901 he assumed editorship of Flower's popular *New Thought* magazine, a post which he held until 1905. During these years, he built for himself an enduring place in the hearts of its readers. Article after article flowed from his pen. Meanwhile, he also founded his own Psychic Club and the so-called "Atkinson School of Mental Science." Both were located in the same building as Flower's Psychic Research and New Thought Publishing Company.

Throughout his subsequent career, Atkinson wrote and published under his own name and many pseudonyms. It is not known whether he ever acknowledged authorship of these pseudonymous works, but all of the supposedly independent authors whose writings are now credited to Atkinson were linked to one another by virtue of the fact that their works were released by a series of publishing houses with shared addresses and they also wrote for a series of magazines with a shared roster of authors. Atkinson was the editor of all of those magazines and his pseudonymous authors acted first as "contributors" to the periodicals, and were then spun off into their own book-writing careers—with most of their books being released by Atkinson's own publishing houses.

One key to unravelling this tangled web of pseudonyms is found in *Advanced Thought* magazine, billed as "A Journal of The New Thought, Practical Psychology, Yogi Philosophy, Constructive Occultism, Metaphysical Healing, Etc."

This magazine, edited by Atkinson, advertised articles by Atkinson, Yogi Ramacharaka, and Theron Q. Dumont—the latter two being pseudonyms of Atkinson—and it had the same address as The Yogi Publishing Society, which published the works attributed to Yogi Ramacharaka.

Advanced Thought magazine also carried articles by Swami Bhakta Vishita, but when it came time for Vishita's writings to be collected in book form, they were not published by the Yogi Publishing Society. Instead they were published by The Advanced Thought Publishing Co., the same house that brought out the Theron Q. Dumont books—and published *Advanced Thought* magazine.

* * * *

In the 1890s, Atkinson had become interested in Hinduism, and after 1900 he devoted a great deal of effort to the diffusion of yoga and Oriental occultism in the West. It is unclear at this late date whether he actually ever converted to any form of Hindu religion, or merely wished to write on the subject. If he did convert, he left no record of the event.

According to unverifiable sources, while Atkinson was in Chicago at the World's Columbian Exposition in 1893, he met one Baba Bharata, a pupil of the late Indian mystic Yogi Ramacharaka (1799 - c.1893). As the story goes, Bharata had become acquainted with Atkinson's writings after arriving in America, the two men shared similar ideas, and so they decided to collaborate. While editing *New Thought* magazine, it is claimed, Atkinson co-wrote with Bharata a series of books which they attributed to Bharata's teacher, Yogi Ramacharaka. This story cannot be verified and—like the "official" biography that falsely claimed Atkinson was an "English author"—it may be a fabrication.

No record exists in India of a Yogi Ramacharaka, nor is there evidence in America of the immigration of a Baba Bharata. Furthermore, although Atkinson may have travelled to Chicago to visit the 1892–1893 World's Columbian Exposition, where the authentic Indian yogi Swami Vivekananda attracted enthusiastic audiences, he is only known to have taken up residence in Chicago around 1900 and to have passed the Illinois Bar Examination in 1903.

Atkinson's claim to have an Indian co-author was actually not unusual among the New Thought and New Age writers of his era. As Carl T. Jackson made clear in his 1975 article "The New Thought Movement and the Nineteenth Century Discovery of Oriental Philosophy," Atkinson was not alone in embracing a vaguely exotic "orientalism" as a running theme in his writing, nor in crediting Hindus, Buddhists, or Sikhs with the possession of special knowledge and secret techniques of clairvoyance, spiritual development, sexual energy, health, or longevity.

The way had been paved in the mid to late 19th century by Paschal Beverly Randolph, who wrote in his books *Eulis* and *Seership* that he had been taught the mysteries of mirror scrying by the deposed Indian Maharajah Dalip Singh. Randolph was known for embroidering the truth when it came to his own autobiography (he claimed that his mother Flora Randolph, an African-American woman from Virginia, who died when he was eleven years old, had been a foreign princess) but he was actually telling the truth—or something very close to it, according to his biographer John Patrick Deveney—when he said that he had met the Maharajah in Europe and had learned from him the proper way to use both polished gemstones and Indian "bhattah mirrors" in divination.

In 1875, the year of Randolph's death, the Ukrainian-born Helena Petrovna Blavatsky founded the Theosophical Society, by means of which she spread the teachings of mysterious Himalayan enlightened yogis, the Masters of the Ancient Wisdom, and the doctrines of the Eastern philosophy in general. After this pioneer work, some representatives from known lineages of Indian and Asian spiritual and philosophical tradition—like Vivekananda, Anagarika Dharmapala, Paramahansa Yogananda, and others—started coming to the West.

In any case, with or without a co-author, Atkinson started writing a series of books under the name Yogi Ramacharaka in 1903, ultimately releasing more than a dozen titles under this pseudonym. The Ramacharaka books were published by the Yogi Publication Society in Chicago and reached more people than Atkinson's New Thought works did. In fact, all of his books on yoga are still in print today.

Atkinson apparently enjoyed the idea of writing as a Hindu so much that he created two more Indian personas, Swami Bhakta Vishita and Swami Panchadasi. Strangely, neither of these identities wrote on Hinduism. Their material was for the most part concerned with the arts of divination and mediumship, including "oriental" forms of clairvoyance and seership. Of the two, Swami Bhakta Vishita was by far the more popular, and with more than 30 titles to his credit, he eventually outsold even Yogi Ramacharaka.

CHAPTER I

WHAT IS THE HUMAN AURA?

The above question is frequently asked the student of occultism by some one who has heard the term but who is unfamiliar with its meaning. Simple as the question may seem, it is by no means easy to answer it, plainly and clearly in a few words, unless the hearer already has a general acquaintance with the subject of occult science. Let us commence at the beginning, and consider the question from the point of view of the person who has just heard the term for the first time.

The dictionaries define the word aura as: "Any subtle, invisible emanation or exhalation." The English authorities, as a rule, attribute the origin of the word to a Latin term meaning "air," but the Hindu authorities insist that it had its origin in the Sanscrit root *Ar*, meaning the spoke of a wheel, the significance being perceived when we remember the fact that the human aura radiates from the body of the individual in a manner similar to the radiation of the spokes of a wheel from the hub thereof. The Sanscrit origin of the term is the one preferred by occultists, although it will be seen that the idea of an aerial emanation, indicated by the Latin root, is not foreign to the real significance of the term.

Be the real origin of the term what it may, the idea of the human aura is one upon which all occultists are in full agreement and harmony, and the mention of which is found in all works upon the general subject of occultism. So we shall begin by a consideration of the main conception thereof, as held by all advanced occultists, ancient and modern, omitting little points of theoretical variance between the different schools.

Briefly, then, the human aura may be described as a fine, ethereal radiation or emanation surrounding each and every living human being. It extends from two to three feet, in all directions, from the body. It assumes an oval shape—a great egg-shaped nebula surrounding the body on all sides for a distance of two or three feet. This aura is sometimes referred to, in ordinary terms, as the "psychic atmosphere" of a person, or as his "magnetic atmosphere."

This atmosphere or aura is apparent to a large percentage of persons in the sense of the psychic awareness generally called "feeling," though the term is not a clear one. The majority of persons are more or less aware of that subtle something about the personality of others, which can be sensed or felt in a clear though unusual way when the other persons are near by, even though they may be out of the range of the vision. Being outside of the ordinary range of the five senses, we are apt to feel that there is something queer or uncanny about these feelings of projected personality. But every person, deep in his heart, knows them to be realities and admits their effect upon his impressions regarding the persons from whom they emanate. Even small children, infants even, perceive this influence, and respond to it in the matter of likes and dislikes.

But, human testimony regarding the existence and character of the human aura does not stop with the reports of the psychic senses to which we have just referred. There are many individuals of the race—a far greater percentage than is generally imagined—who have the gift of psychic sight more or less developed. Many persons have quite a well-developed power of this kind, who do not mention it to their acquaintances for fear of ridicule, or of being thought "queer." In addition to these persons, there are here and there to be found well-developed, clear-sighted, or truly clairvoyant persons, whose powers of psychic perception are as highly developed as are the ordinary senses of the average individual. And, the reports of these persons, far apart in time and space though they may be, have always agreed on the main points of psychic phenomena, particularly in regards to the human aura.

To the highly developed clairvoyant vision, every human being is seen as surrounded by the egg-shaped aura of two or three feet in depth, more dense and thick in the portion nearest the body, and then gradually becoming more tenuous, thin and indistinct as the distance from the body is increased. By the psychic perception, the aura is seen as a luminous cloud—a phosphorescent flame—deep and dense around the centre and then gradually shading into indistinctness toward the edges. As a matter of fact, as all developed occultists know, the aura really extends very much further than even the best clairvoyant vision can perceive it, and its psychic influence is perceptible at quite a distance in many cases. In this respect it is like any flame on the physical plane—it gradually fades into indistinctness, its rays persisting far beyond the reach of the vision, as may be proved by means of chemical apparatus, etc.

To the highly developed clairvoyant vision, the human aura is seen to be composed of all the colors of the spectrum, the combinations of colors differing in various persons, and constantly shifting in the case of every person. These colors reflect the mental (particularly the emotional) states of the person in whose aura they are manifested. Each mental state has its own particular combination formed from the few elementary colors which represent the elementary mental conditions. As the mind is ever shifting and changing its states, it follows that there will ever be a corresponding series of shifting changes in the colors of the human aura.

The shades and colors of the aura present an ever changing kaleidoscopic spectacle, of wonderful beauty and most interesting character. The trained occultist is able to read the character of any person, as well as the nature of his passing thoughts and feelings, by simply studying the shifting colors of his aura. To the developed occultist the mind and character become as an open book, to be studied carefully and intelligently.

Even the student of occultism, who has not been able to develop the clairvoyant vision to such a high degree, is soon able to develop the sense of psychic perception whereby he is able to at least "feel" the vibrations of the aura, though he may not see the colors, and thus be able to interpret the mental states which have caused them. The principle is of course the same, as the colors are but the outward appearance of the vibrations themselves, just as the ordinary colors on the physical plane are merely the outward manifestation of vibration of matter.

But it must not be supposed that the human aura is always perceived in the appearance of a luminous cloud of ever-changing color. When we say that such is its characteristic appearance, we mean it in the same sense that we describe the ocean as a calm, deep body of greenish waters. We know, however, that at times the ocean presents no such appearance, but, instead, is seen as rising in great mountainous waves, white capped, and threatening the tiny vessels of men with its power. Or again, we may define the word "flame" in the sense of a steady bright stream of burning gas, whereas, we know only too well, that the word also indicates the great hot tongues of fiery force that stream out from the windows of a burning building, and lick to destruction all with which it comes in contact.

So it is with the human aura. At times it may be seen as a beautiful, calm, luminous atmosphere, presenting the appearance of a great opal under the rays of the sun. Again, it blazes like the flames of a great furnace, shooting forth great tongues of fire in this direction and that, rising and falling in great waves of emotional excitement, or passion, or perhaps whirling like a great fiery maelstrom toward its centre, or swirling in an outward movement away from its centre. Again it may be seen as projecting from its depths smaller bodies or centres of mental vibration, which like sparks from a furnace detach themselves from the parent flame, and travel far away in other directions—these are the projected thought-forms of which all occultists are fond of speaking and which make plain many strange psychic occurrences.

So, it will be seen, the human aura is a very important and interesting phase of the personality of every individual. The psychic phase of man is as much the man himself as is the physical phase—the complete man being made up of the two phases. Man invisible is as much the real man as is man visible. As the finer forms of nature are always the most powerful, so is the psychic man more potent than the physical man.

In this book, I speak of the human aura, and its colors, as being perceived by astral or clairvoyant vision, for this is the way in which it is perceived and studied by the occultist. The occult teaching is that, in the evolution of the race, this astral vision will eventually become the common property of every human being—it so exists even now, and needs only development to perfect it.

But modern physical science is today offering corroborative proof (though the same is not needed by the occultist who has the astral vision) to the general public, of the existence of the human aura. In Europe, especially, a number of scientists have written on the subject of the aura, and have described the result of the experiments in which the aura has been perceived, and even photographed, by means of fluorescent screens, such as are used in taking X-Ray photographs, etc. Leading authorities in England, France, and still more recently, in Germany, have reported the discovery (!) of a nebulous, hazy, radio-active energy or substance, around the body of human beings. In short, they now claim that every human being is radio-active, and that the auric radiation may be registered and perceived by means of a screen composed of certain fluorescent material, interposed between the eye of the observer, and the person observed.

This aura, so discovered (!) by the scientists, is called by them the "human atmosphere," and is classified by them as similar to the radiations of other radio-active substances, radium, for instance. They have failed to discover color in this atmosphere, however, and know nothing, apparently, of the relation between auric colors and mental and emotional states, which are so familiar to every advanced occultist. I mention this fact merely as a matter of general interest and information to the student, and not as indicating, even in the slightest degree, any idea on my part that the old occult teaching, and the observed phenomena accompanying the same, regarding the human aura, require any proof or backing up on the part of material scientists. On the contrary, I feel that material science should feel flattered by the backing up by occult science of the new discovery (!) of the "human atmosphere." A little later on, material science may also discover (!) the auric colors, and announce the same to the wondering world, as a new truth.

CHAPTER II

THE PRANA-AURA

Many writers on the subject of the human aura content themselves with a description of the colors of the mental or emotional aura, and omit almost any reference whatsoever to the basic substance or power of the aura. This is like the play of Hamlet, with the character of Hamlet omitted, for, unless we understand something concerning the fundamental substance of which the aura is composed, we cannot expect to arrive at a clear understanding of the phenomena which arises from and by reason of the existence of this fundamental substance. We might as well expect a student to understand the principles of color, without having been made acquainted with the principles of light.

The fundamental substance of which the human aura is composed is none other than that wonderful principle of nature of which one reads so much in all occult writings, which has been called by many names, but which is perhaps best known under the Sanscrit term, *Prana*, but which may be thought of as Vital Essence, Life Power, etc.

It is not necessary in this book to go into the general consideration of the nature and character of Prana. It is sufficient for us to consider it in its manifestation of Vital Force, Life Essence, etc. In its broadest sense, Prana really is the Principle of Energy in Nature, but in its relation to living forms it is the Vital Force which lies at the very basis of manifested Life. It exists in all forms of living things, from the most minute microscopic form up to living creatures on higher planes, as much higher than man as man is higher than the simple microscopic life-forms. It permeates them all, and renders possible all life activity and functioning.

Prana is not the mind or the soul, but is rather the force or energy through which the soul manifests activity, and the mind manifests thought. It is the steam that runs the physical and mental machinery of life. It is the substance of the human aura, and the colors of mental states are manifested in that substance, just as the colors of chemical bodies are manifested in the substance of water. But Prana is not material substance—it is higher than mere matter, being the underlying substance of Energy or Force in Nature.

While it is true, as we have seen, that all auras are composed of the substance of Prana, it is likewise true that there is a simple and elementary form of auric substance to which occultists have given the simple name of the prana-aura in order to distinguish it from the more complex forms and phases of the human aura. The simplicity of the character of the prana-aura causes it to be more readily sensed or perceived than is possible in the case of the more complex phases or forms of the aura. For whereas it is only the more sensitive organisms that can distinguish the finer vibrations of the mental and emotional aura, and only the clairvoyant sight which can discern its presence by its colors, almost any person, by a little careful experimenting, may become aware of the presence of the prana-aura, not only in the way of "feeling" it, but in many cases of actually seeing it with the ordinary vision rightly directed.

That which is known as the prana-aura is of course the most simple form or phase of the human aura. It is the form or phase which is more closely bound up with the physical body, and is less concerned with the mental states. This fact has caused some writers to speak of it as the "health aura," or "physical aura," both of which terms are fittingly applied as we shall see, although we prefer the simpler term we have used here, i. e., the prana-aura. For the prana-aura does show the state of the health of the individual radiating it, and it also really contains physical power and magnetism which may be, and is imparted to others.

The basic prana-aura is practically colorless, that is to say, it is about the color of the clearest water or a very clear diamond. By the clairvoyant vision it is seen to be streaked or marked by very minute, bristle-like lines, radiating outward from the physical body of the individual, in a manner very like "the quills upon the fretful porcupine," as Shakespeare puts it. In the case of excellent physical health, these bristle-like streaks are stiff and brittle-looking, whereas, if the general health of the person be deficient these bristle-like radiations seem to be more or less tangled, twisted, or curly; and, in some cases present a drooping appearance, and in extreme cases present the appearance of soft, limp fur.

It may interest the student to know that minute particles of this prana-aura, or vital magnetism, is sloughed off the body in connection with physical exhalations such as scent, etc., and remain in existence for some time after the person has passed from the particular place at which they were cast off. In fact, as all occultists know, it is these particles of the prana-aura which serve to give vitality to the "scent" of living creatures, which enables dogs and other animals to trace up the track of the person, or animal, for a long time after the person has passed. It is not alone the physical odor, which must be very slight as you will see upon a moment's consideration. It is really the presence of the particles of the prana-aura which enables the dog to distinguish the traces of one person among that of thousands of others, and the feat is as much psychical as physical.

Another peculiarity of the prana-aura is that it is filled with a multitude of extremely minute sparkling particles, resembling tiny electric sparks, which are in constant motion. These sparks, which are visible to persons of only slightly developed psychic power, impart a vibratory motion to the prana-aura which, under certain conditions is plainly visible to the average person. This vibratory movement is akin to the movement of heated air arising from a hot stove, or from the heated earth on a mid-summer day.

If the student will close his eyes partially, until he peers out from narrowed lids, and then will closely observe some very healthy person sitting in a dim light, he may perceive this undulating, pulsing vibration extending an inch or two from the surface of the body. It requires some little knack to recognize these vibrations, but a little practice will often give one the key; and after the first recognition, the matter becomes easy.

Again, in the case of persons of active brains, one may perceive this pulsating prana-aura around the head of the person, particularly when he is engaged in concentrated active thought. A little practice will enable almost any one to perceive faintly the dim outlines of the prana-aura around his own fingers and hand, by placing his hand against a black background, in a dim light, and then gazing at it with narrowed eye-lids, squinting if necessary. Under these circumstances, after a little practice, one will be apt to perceive a tiny outlined aura, or radiation, or halo, of pale yellowish light surrounding the hand.

By extending the fingers, fan shape, you will perceive that each finger is showing its own little outlined prana-aura. The stronger the vital force, the plainer will be the perception of the phenomenon. Often the prana-aura, in these experiments, will appear like the semi-luminous radiance surrounding a candle flame or gas light. Under the best conditions, the radiation will assume an almost phosphorescent appearance. Remember, this is simply a matter of trained ordinary sight,—not clairvoyant vision.

This prana-aura is identical with human magnetism, which is employed in ordinary magnetic healing. That is to say it is the outer manifestation of the wonderful pranic force. It is felt when you shake hands, or otherwise come in close physical contact with a strongly magnetic person. On the other hand it is what the weakly, human vampire-like persons unconsciously, or consciously, try to draw off from strong persons, if the latter allow them so to do from want of knowledge of self protection. Who has not met persons of this kind, who seem to sap one's very life force away from him? Remember, then, that the prana-aura is the aura or radiation of life force, or vital power, which is the steam of your living activity, physical and mental. It is the pouring out of the vital "steam" which is running your vital machinery. Its presence indicates Life—its absence Lifelessness.

CHAPTER III

THE ASTRAL COLORS

The term "astral," so frequently employed by all occultists, is difficult to explain or define except to those who have pursued a regular course of study in occult science. For the purpose of the present consideration, it is enough to say that over and above the ordinary physical sense plane there is another and more subtle plane, known as the Astral Plane. Every human being possesses the innate and inherent faculty of sensing the things of this astral plane, by means of an extension or enlargement of the powers of the ordinary senses, so to speak. But, in the majority of persons in the present stage of development, these astral senses are lying dormant, and only here and there do we find individuals who are able to sense on the astral plane, although in the course of evolution the entire race will be able to do so, of course. The colors of the human aura, mentioned in the preceding two chapters, and which arise from the various mental and emotional states, belong to the phenomena of the astral plane, and hence bear the name of "the astral colors." Belonging to the astral plane, and not to the ordinary physical plane, they are perceived only by the senses functioning on the astral plane, and are invisible to the ordinary physical plane sight. But, to those who have developed the astral sight, or clairvoyance, these colors are as real as are the ordinary colors to the average person, and their phenomena have been as carefully recorded by occult science as have the physical plane colors by physical science. The fact that to the ordinary physical senses they are invisible, does not render them any the less real. Remember, in this connection, that to the blind man our physical colors do not exist. And, for that matter, the ordinary colors do not exist to "color blind" persons. The ordinary physical plane person is simply "color blind" to the astral colors—that's all.

On the astral plane each shade of mental or emotional state has its corresponding astral color, the latter manifesting when the form appears. It follows then, of course, that when once the occultist has the key to this color correspondence, and thus is able to perceive the astral colors by means of his astral vision, he also is able to read the mental and emotional states of any person within the range of his vision, as easily as you are now reading the printed words of this book.

Before proceeding to a consideration of the list of astral colors in the human aura, I wish to call your attention to a slight variation in the case of the prana-aura, of which I have spoken in our last chapter. I have stated therein that the prana-aura is colorless like a diamond or clear water. This is true in the average case, but in the case of a person of very strong physical vitality or virility, the prana-aura takes on, at times, a faint warm pink tinge, which is really a reflection from the red astral color, of the meaning of which color you shall now learn.

Like their physical plane counterparts, all the astral colors are formed from three Primary Colors, namely (1) Red; (2) Blue; and (3) Yellow. From these three primary colors, all other colors are formed. Following the Primary Colors, we find what are known as the Secondary Colors, namely: (1) Green, derived from a combination of Yellow and Blue; (2) Orange, formed from a combination of Yellow and Red; and (3) Purple, formed from a combination of Red and Blue. Further combinations produce the other colors, as for instance, Green and Purple form Olive; Orange and Purple form Russet; Green and Orange form Citrine.

Black is called an absence of color, while White is really a harmonious blending of all colors, strange as this may appear to one who has not studied the subject. The blending of the Primary Colors in varied proportions produce what is known as the "hues" of color. Adding white to the hues, we obtain "tints;" while mixing Black produces "shades." Strictly speaking Black and White are known as "neutral" colors.

Now for the meaning of the astral colors—that is, the explanation of the mental or emotional state represented by each. I ask that the student familiarize himself with the meaning of the Primary Colors and their combinations. A clear understanding of the key of the astral colors is often an aid in the development of astral sight.

KEY TO THE ASTRAL COLORS

RED. Red represents the physical phase of mentality. That is to say, it stands for that part of the mental activities which are concerned with physical life. It is manifested by the vitality of the body, and in other hues, tints and shades, is manifested by passions, anger, physical cravings, etc. I shall describe the various forms of Red manifestation, a little later on.

BLUE. Blue represents the religious, or spiritual, phase of mentality. That is to say, it stands for that part of the mental activities which are concerned with high ideals, altruism, devotion, reverence, veneration, etc. It is manifested, in its various hues, tints, and shades, by all forms of religious feeling and emotion, high and low, as we shall see as we proceed.

YELLOW. Yellow represents the intellectual phase of mentality. That is to say, it stands for that part of the mental activities which are concerned with reasoning, analysis, judgment, logical processes, induction, deduction, synthesis, etc. In its various hues, tints and shades, it is manifested by the various forms of intellectual activity, high and low, as we shall see as we proceed.

WHITE. White stands for what occultists know as Pure Spirit, which is a very different thing from the religious emotion of "spirituality," and which really is the essence of the ALL that really is. Pure Spirit is the positive pole of Being. We shall see the part played by it in the astral colors, as we proceed.

BLACK. Black stands for the negative pole of Being—the very negation of Pure Spirit, and opposing it in every way. We shall see the part played by it in the astral colors as we proceed.

The various combinations of the three Astral Primary Colors are formed in connection with Black and White as well as by the blending of the three themselves. These combinations, of course, result from the shades of mental and emotional activity manifested by the individuality, of which they are the reflection and the key.

The combinations and blending of the astral colors, however, are numberless, and present an almost infinite variety. Not only is the blending caused by the mixing of the colors themselves, in connection with black and white, but in many cases the body of one color is found to be streaked, striped, dotted or clouded by other colors. At times there is perceived the mixture of two antagonistic color streams fighting against each other before blending. Again we see the effect of one color neutralizing another.

In some cases great black clouds obscure the bright colors beneath, and then darken the fierce glow of color, just as is often witnessed in the case of a physical conflagration. Again, we find great flashes of bright yellow, or red, flaring across the field of the aura, showing agitation or the conflict of intellect and passion.

The average student, who has not developed the astral vision, is inclined to imagine that the astral colors in the human aura present the appearance of an egg-shaped rainbow, or spectrum, or something of that sort. But this is a great mistake. In the first place, the astral colors are seldom at rest, for all mental and emotional activity is the result of vibration, change, and rhythmic motion. Consequently, the colors of the aura present a kaleidoscopic appearance, of constant change of color, shape and grouping—a great electrical display, so to speak, constantly shifting, changing, and blending.

Great tongues of flamelike emanations project themselves beyond the border of the aura, under strong feeling or excitement, and great vibratory whirls and swirls are manifested. The sight is most fascinating, although somewhat terrifying at first. Nature is wise in bestowing the gift of astral vision only gradually and by almost imperceptible stages of advance. There are many unpleasant, as well as pleasant, sights on the Astral Plane.

CHAPTER IV

THE ASTRAL COLORS (CONTINUED)

Remembering, always, the significance of the three primary colors on the astral plane, let us consider the meaning of the combinations, shades, hues, and tints of these colors.

THE RED GROUP. In this group of astral colors seen in the human aura, we find strongly in evidence the clear bright red shade, similar to that of fresh, pure arterial blood as it leaves the heart, filled with pure material freshly oxygenated. This shade, in the aura, indicates health, life-force, vigor, virility, etc., in pure and untainted form. The aura of a healthy, strong child shows this shade of color very plainly and strongly.

Strong, pure natural emotions, such as friendship, love of companionship, love of physical exercise, healthy clean sports, etc., are manifested by a clear clean shade of red. When these feelings become tainted with selfishness, low motives, etc., the shade grows darker and duller. Love of low companionship, unclean sports, or selfish games, etc., produce an unpleasant muddy red shade.

A shade of red, very near to crimson, is the astral color of Love, but the tint and shade varies greatly according to the nature of this form of emotional feeling. A very high form of love, which seeks the good of the loved one, rather than the satisfaction of oneself, manifests as a beautiful rose tint—one of the most pleasing of the astral tints, by the way. Descending in the scale, we find the crimson shade becoming darker and duller, until we descend to the plane of impure, sensual, coarse passion, which is manifested by an ugly, dull, muddy crimson of a repulsive appearance, suggesting blood mixed with dirty earth or barnyard soil.

A peculiar series of red shades are those manifesting anger in its various forms, from the vivid scarlet flashes of anger color, arising from what may be called "righteous indignation," down the scale to the ugly flashes of deep, dull red, betokening rage and uncontrolled passion. The red of anger generally shows itself in flashes, or great leaping flames, often accompanied by a black background, in the case of malicious hate, or by a dirty, greenish background when the rage arises from jealousy, or envy. The color of avarice is a very ugly combination of dull, dark red, and a dirty ugly green. If persons could see their own astral colors accompanying these undesirable mental states, the sight would perhaps so disgust them with such states as to work a cure. At any rate, they are most disgusting and repulsive to the occultist who beholds them in the human aura, and he often wonders why they do not sicken the person manifesting them—they often do just this thing, to tell the truth.

THE YELLOW GROUP. In this group of astral colors seen in the human aura we find as many varieties as we do in the red group. Yellow, denoting intellect, has many degrees of shade and tint, and many degrees of clearness.

An interesting shade in this group is that of Orange, which represents different forms of "pride of intellect," intellectual ambition, love of mastery by will, etc. The greater degree of red in the astral orange color, the greater the connection with the physical or animal nature. Pride and love of power over others, has much red in its astral color, while love of intellectual mastery has much less red in its composition.

Pure intellectual attainment, and the love of the same, is manifested by a beautiful clear golden yellow. Great teachers often have this so strongly in evidence, that at times their students have glimpses of a golden "halo" around the head of the teacher. Teachers of great spirituality have this "nimbus" of golden yellow, with a border of beautiful blue tint, strongly in evidence.

The paintings of the great spiritual teachers of the race usually have this radiance pictured as a "halo," showing a recognition of the phenomenon on the part of the great artists. Hoffman's celebrated painting of the Christ in the Garden of Gethsemane shows this nimbus so accurately depicted that the occultist is convinced that this artist must have actually witnessed a similar scene in the astral light, so true to the astral facts are its details. The images of the Buddha also show this radiance.

The rich golden shades of intellectual yellow are comparatively rare, a sickly lemon color being the only indication of intellectual power and found in the aura of the great run of persons. To the sight of the occultist, employing his power of astral vision, a crowd of persons will manifest here and there, at widely separated points, the bright golden yellow of the true intellect, appearing like scattered lighted candles among a multitude of faintly burning matches.

THE GREEN GROUP. This is a peculiar group, consisting as of course it does of various combinations of blues and yellows, tinted and shaded by white or black. Even skilled occultists find it very difficult to account for the fact of certain green shades arising from the spiritual blue and the intellectual yellow—this is one of the most obscure points in the whole subject of the astral colors, and none but the most advanced occultists are able to explain the "why" in some instances. To those who are fond of analysis of this kind, I will drop the following hint, which may help them out in the matter, viz. The key is found in the fact that Green lies in the centre of the astral spectrum, and is a balance between the two extremes, and is also influenced by these two extremes in a startling manner.

A certain restful green denotes love of nature, out of door life, travel in the country, etc., and also, slightly differing in tint, the love of home scenes, etc. Again, a clear beautiful lighter tint of green indicates what may be called sympathy, altruistic emotion, charity, etc. Again, illustrating variety in this group of astral colors, another shade of green shows intellectual tolerance of the views of others. Growing duller, this indicates tact, diplomacy, ability to handle human nature, and descending another degree or so blends into insincerity, shiftiness, untruth, etc. There is an ugly slate-colored green indicating low, tricky deceit—this is a very common shade in the colors of the average aura, I am sorry to say. Finally, a particularly ugly, muddy, murky green indicates jealousy and kindred feelings, envious malice, etc.

THE BLUE GROUP. This interesting group of astral colors represents the varying forms and degrees of religious emotion, "spirituality," etc. The highest form of spiritual, religious feeling and thought is represented by a beautiful, rich, clear violet tint, while the lower and more gross phases of religious emotion and thought are represented by the darker and duller hues, tints, and shades until a deep, dark indigo is reached, so dark that it can scarcely be distinguished from a bluish black. This latter color, as might be expected, indicates a low superstitious form of religion, scarcely worthy of the latter name. Religion, we must remember, has its low places as well as its heights—its garden grows the rarest flowers, and at the same time the vilest weeds.

High spiritual feelings—true spiritual unfoldment—is indicated by a wonderfully clear light blue, of an unusual tint, something akin to the clear light blue of the sky on a cool autumn afternoon, just before sunset. Even when we witness an approach to this color in Nature, we are inspired by an uplifting feeling as if we were in the presence of higher things, so true is the intuition regarding these things.

Morality, of a high degree, is indicated by a series of beautiful shades of blue, always of a clear inspiring tint. Religious feeling ruled by fear, is indicated by a shade of bluish gray. Purple denotes a love of form and ceremony, particularly those connected with religious offices or regal grandeur of a solemn kind. Purple, naturally, was chosen as the royal color in the olden days.

THE BROWN GROUP. The brown group of astral colors represents desire for gain and accumulation, ranging from the clear brown of industrious accumulation, to the murky dull browns of miserliness, greed and avarice. There is a great range in this group of brown shades, as may be imagined.

THE GRAY GROUP. The group of grays represents a negative group of thought and emotions. Gray represents fear, depression, lack of courage, negativity, etc. This is an undesirable and unpleasant group.

BLACK. Black, in the astral colors, stands for hatred, malice, revenge, and "devilishness" generally. It shades the brighter colors into their lower aspects, and robs them of their beauty. It stands for hate—also for gloom, depression, pessimism, etc.

WHITE. White is the astral color of Pure Spirit, as we have seen, and its presence raises the degree of the other colors, and renders them clearer. In fact, the perception of the highest degree of Being known to the most advanced occultist is manifested to the highest adepts and masters in the form of "The Great White Light," which transcends any light ever witnessed by the sight of man on either physical or astral plane—for it belongs to a plane higher than either, and is absolute, rather than a relative, white. The presence of white among the astral colors of the human aura, betokens a high degree of spiritual attainment and unfoldment, and when seen permeating the entire aura it is one of the Signs of the Master—the token of Adeptship.

CHAPTER V

THE AURIC KALEIDOSCOPE

As we have seen, the human aura is never in a state of absolute rest or quiet. Motion and change is ever manifested by it. It has its periods of comparative calm, of course, but even in this state there is a pulsing, wave-like motion apparent. The clouds of changing color fly over its surface, and in its depth, like the fast driven fleecy clouds over the summer sky, illumined by the rays of the setting sun.

Again, fierce storms of mental activity, or emotional stress, disturb its comparative calm, and the wildest scenes are witnessed in the aura by the observer. So intense are the vibrations of some of these mental storms that their effect is plainly felt by the average person, though he is not able to distinguish the colors or the great whirls and swirls of auric substance accompanying them.

A person sunk in reverie, dream-states, or sleep, presents an interesting auric kaleidoscope, which possesses great beauty if the person be normal and of average morality. In such a case there is a cloudy-clearness (if the term may be used) tinged with tints and shades of varying colors, blending in strange and interesting combinations, appearing gradually from previous combinations, and sinking gradually into new ones.

To the observer of the aura the term "opalescent" instinctly presents itself, for there is a striking resemblance to the opaline peculiar play of colors of delicate tints and shades in a body of pearly or milky hue. Color shades into color, tint into tint, hue into hue, as in the color scale of the spectrum of which the rainbow is the most familiar example. But the rainbow or spectrum lacks the peculiar semi-transparency of the auric colors, and also the constantly changing and dissolving body of colors of the aura.

At this point, I wish to call your attention to a phase of the aura which I purposely passed over in the preceding chapters. I allude to the phase of the aura which presents the "pearly" appearance of the opalescent body, which we have just noted. This appearance is manifested neither by any of the mental or emotional states, nor is it the prana-aura or vital force which I have described in a previous chapter. It is the manifestation of what is known to occultists as "etheric substance," and is a very interesting feature of the auric phenomena.

This etheric substance, which manifests this peculiar radiance in the body of the aura, composes that which is called by some occultists "the astral body," but this latter term is also employed in another sense, and I prefer to use the term "etheric double" to indicate what some others know as "the astral body." Etheric substance is much finer form of substance than that which composes the physical body. It is really matter in a very high degree of vibration—much higher than even the ultra-gaseous matter of physical substance. It may be sensed, ordinarily, only on the astral plane, which is its own particular plane of activity.

The etheric double, composed of this etheric substance, is the exact counterpart of its physical counterpart—the ordinary physical body of the individual—although it is capable of great expansion or shrinking in space. Like the physical body it radiates an aura, and this combining with the other forms of the auric body, gives to it its peculiar pearly appearance, which is the background of its opalescence previously noted.

The etheric double explains the phenomenon of spectral appearances or ghosts, for it persists for a time after the death of the physical body, and under some conditions becomes visible to the ordinary sight. It sometimes is projected from the physical body, and at such times appears as an apparition of the living, of which there are many cases recorded by the societies investigating psychical subjects.

The etheric double, or astral body, is referred to here, however, merely to explain the peculiar pearly tint of the background, or body, of the aura, in and through which the mental and emotional auric colors play and move. It may interest you, however, to know that this phase of aura is always present around and about a "ghost" or dematerialized disembodied soul, or "spirit" as common usage terms it.

The aura of the wide-awake person is, of course, far more active and more deeply colored than is that of the person in reverie, dream, or sleep. And, again the aura of the person manifesting a high degree of mental activity, or strong feeling or passion, is still brighter and deeper than the ordinary person performing his daily routine work. In the state of anger, or love-passion, for instance, the aura is violently disturbed, deep shades of color whirling and swirling in the depths and surface of the auric body. Lightning-like flashes shoot forth and great bodies of lurid smoky clouds fly on the surface. Looking into the aura of a man wild with rage and passion, is like peering into Inferno. The astral plane, in the region of a lynching mob, or other body of persons filled with rage, becomes a frightful scene of auric radiation.

A person filled with the emotion of pure love, fills his aura with the most beautiful tints and shades of high rosy color, and to behold the same is a pleasure fully appreciated by the occultist. A church filled with persons of a high devotional ideality, is also a beautiful place, by reason of the mingling of auric violet-blue vibrations of those therein assembled. The atmosphere of a prison is most depressing and presents a most unpleasant appearance to one possessing the astral vision. Likewise the astral atmosphere of an abode of vice and passion, becomes really physically nauseating to the occultist of high ideals and taste. Such scenes on the astral plane are avoided by all true occultists, except when the call of duty leads them to visit them to give aid and help.

There are two distinct features connected with the auric coloring of every person. The first is the coloring resulting from the more habitual thoughts and feelings of the person—from his character, in fact; while the second is the coloring resulting from the particular feelings, or thoughts, manifested by him at that particular moment or time.

The color of the feeling of the moment soon disappears and fades away, while the more habitual feeling, bound up with his character, causes its corresponding color to abide more permanently, and thus to give a decided hue to his general auric color appearance.

The trained occultist is, therefore, able to ascertain not only the passing thoughts and feelings of a person, but also to determine infallibly his general character, tendencies, past character and actions, and general nature, simply from a careful examination and study of the auric colors of the person in question.

As all occultists well know, every place, dwelling, business place, church, courtroom—every village, city, country, nation—has its own collective aura, known as "astral atmosphere," which is simply but a combined reflection of the individual auras of the human units of which its body of inhabitants is made up. These atmospheric vibrations are plainly felt by many persons, and we are instinctively attracted or repelled by reason thereof. But, to the developed occultists, these places manifest the auric colors, in the combinations arising from the nature of the mentalities of the persons dwelling in them.

Each place has its collective aura, just as each person has his individual aura. The astral plane presents a wonderful scene of color by reason of this and similar causes. The harmony of the color scheme, in some cases, is marvellously beautiful; while the horrible aspect of scenes resemble a nightmare vision of the worst kind.

It is easy to understand why some of the ancients who stumbled into glimpses of the astral plane, while in dream-state or trance, reported the vision of terrible hells of unquenchable fire, fiery lakes of smoking brimstone, etc., for such ideas would naturally come to the mind of the uninformed person who had peered into the astral plane in such cases.

And, in the same way, the visions of heaven reported by the saints, and others of high spirituality, are explainable on the theory that these persons had sensed some of the beautiful scenes of the higher astral planes, filled with the combined auric tints and hues of souls of high development. The principle of auric colors holds good on all the many planes of being and existence—high as well as low.

I merely hint at a great occult truth in making the above statements. The thoughtful will be able to read between my lines. I have given you a little key which will unlock the door of many mysteries, if you will but use it intelligently.

CHAPTER VI

THOUGHT FORMS

That interesting phase of occult phenomena, known as "thought forms," is so closely related to the general subject of the human aura that a mention of one must naturally lead to the thought of the other. Thought-forms are built up of the very material composing the aura, and manifest all of the general characteristics thereof, even to the auric colors. An understanding of the facts of the human aura is necessary for a correct understanding of the nature of the thought-forms composed of the same substance.

A "thought form" is a peculiar manifestation of mental activity on the astral plane. It is more than a powerful disturbance in the body of the human aura, although this is the place of its embodiment or birth in the objective world. It is formed in the following manner: A person manifests a strong desire, feeling or idea, which is naturally filled with the dynamic force of his will. This sets up a series of strong vibrations in the body of the aura, which gradually resolve themselves into a strong whirling centre of thought-force involved in a mass of strongly cohesive auric substance, and strongly charged with the power of the prana of the person.

In some cases these thought forms survive in the auric body for some little time, and then gradually fade away. In other cases they survive and maintain an almost independent existence for some time, and exert a strong influence upon other persons coming in the presence of the person. Again, these thought forms may be so strongly charged with prana, and so imbued with the mental force of the person, that they will actually be thrown off and away from the aura itself, and travel in space until they exhaust their initial energy—in the meantime exerting an influence upon the psychic aura of other persons.

A thought-form is more than merely a strongly manifested thought—it really is such a thought, but surrounded by a body of ethereal substance, charged with prana, and even carrying with it the vibration of the life energy of its creator. It is a child of the mind of its creator, and acquires a portion of his life-essence, so to speak, which abides with it for a longer or shorter time after its birth. In extreme instances it becomes practically a semi-living elemental force, of necessarily comparatively short life.

To those who find it difficult to understand how a thought-form can persist after separation from the presence of the thinker, I would say that the phenomena is similar to that of light traveling in space, long after the star which originated it has been destroyed. Or, again, it is like the vibrations of heat remaining in a room after the lamp or stove causing it has been removed, or the fire in the grate having died out. Or like the sound waves of the drum-beat persisting after the beat itself has ceased. It is all a matter of the persistence of vibrations.

Thought forms differ greatly one from the other in the matter of shape and general appearance. The most common and simple form is that of an undulating wave, or series of tiny waves, resembling the circles caused by the dropping of a pebble into a still pond. Another form is that of a tiny rotating bit of cloud-like substance, sometimes whirling towards a central point, like a whirlpool; and sometimes swirling away from the central point like the familiar "pin-wheel" fireworks toy. Another form is akin the ring of smoke projected from the coughing locomotive, or the rounded lips of the cigar smoker, the movement in this kind being a form of spiral rotation. Other thought forms have the appearance of swiftly rotating balls of cloudy substance, often glowing with a faint phosphorescence.

Sometimes the thought form will appear as a great slender jet, like steam ejected from the spout of a tea-kettle, which is sometimes broken up into a series of short, puffed-out jets, each following the jet preceding it, and traveling in a straight line. Sometimes the thought form shoots forth like a streak of dim light, almost resembling a beam of light flashed from a mirror. Occasionally, it will twist its way along like a long, slender corkscrew, or auger, boring into space.

In cases of thought-forms sent forth by explosive emotion, the thought form will actually take the form of a bomb, which literally explodes when it reaches the presence of the person toward whom it is aimed. Every person has experienced this feeling of a thought bomb having been exploded in his near vicinity, having been directed by a vigorous personality. This form is frequently found in the thought forms sent out by a strong, earnest, vigorous orator.

There are strong thought forms which seem to strive to push back the other person, so correctly do they represent the idea and feeling back of their manifestation. Others seem to strive to wind around the other person, and to try to literally drag him toward the first person, this form often accompanying strong appeal, persuasion, coaxing, etc., when accompanied by strong desire. A particularly vigorous form of this kind of thought form takes on the appearance of a nebulous octopus, with long, winding, clinging tentacles, striving to wrap around the other person, and to draw him toward the center.

The force of the feeling behind the manifestation of the thought form will often travel a long distance from the sender—in fact, in cases of great power of concentration, space seems to be no barrier to its passage. In striking instances of thought transference, etc., it will be found that thought forms play an important part.

The variety of shapes of thought forms is almost endless. Each combination of thought and feeling creates its own form, and each individual seems to have his own peculiarities in this respect. The forms I have above described, however, will serve as typical cases to illustrate the more common classes of appearances. The list, however, might be indefinitely expanded from the experience of any experienced occultist, and is not intended to be full by any means. All varieties of geometrical forms are found among the thought forms, some of them being of remarkable beauty.

In considering the subject of projected thought forms, moreover, it must be remembered that they partake of, and manifest, the same colors as does the aura itself, for they are composed of the same material and are charged with the same energy. But, note this difference, that whereas the aura is energized from the constant battery of the organism of the individual, the thought form, on the contrary, has at its service only the energy with which it was charged when it was thrown off—being a storage battery, as it were, which in time expends all of its power and then is powerless.

Every thought form bears the same color that it would possess if it had been retained in the body of the aura itself. But, as a rule, the colors are plainer, and less blended with others—this because each thought form is the representation of a single definite feeling or thought, or group of same, instead of being a body of widely differing mental vibrations. Thus the thought form of anger will show its black and red, with its characteristic flashes. The thought form of passion will show forth its appropriate auric colors and general characteristics. The thought form of high ideal love will show its beautiful form and harmonious tinting, like a wonderful celestial flower from the garden of some far off Paradise.

Many thought forms never leave the outer limits of the aura, while others are projected to great distances. Some sputter out as they travel, and are disintegrated, while others continue to glow like a piece of heated iron, for many hours. Others persist for a long time, with a faint phosphorescent glow. A careful study of what has been said regarding the characteristics of the various feelings and emotions, as manifested in the auric body, will give the student a very fair general idea of what may be the appearance of any particular variety of thought form, for a general principle runs through the entire series of auric phenomena. An understanding of the fundamental principles will lead to an understanding of any of the particular varieties of the manifestation thereof.

Finally, remember this: A thought form is practically a bit of the detached aura of a person, charged with a degree of his prana, and energized with a degree of his life energy. So, in a limited sense, it really is a projected portion of his personality.

CHAPTER VII

PSYCHIC INFLUENCE OF COLORS

In all of Nature's wonderful processes we find many evidences of that great principle of Action and Reaction, which, like the forward and backward swing of the pendulum, changes cause into effect, and effect into cause, in a never ending series. We find this principle in effect in the psychic relation of mental states and colors. That is to say, that just as we find that certain mental and emotional states manifest in vibrations causing particular auric astral colors, so do we find that the presence of certain colors on the physical plane will have a decided psychic effect upon the mental and emotional states of individuals subject to their influence. And, as might be expected by the thoughtful student, the particular astral colors manifested in the aura by the presence of some particular mental or emotional state exactly correspond with the particular physical colors which influence that particular mental or emotional state.

Illustrating the statements in the preceding paragraph, I would say that the continued presence of red will be apt to set up emotional vibrations of anger, passion, physical love, etc., or, in a different tint, the higher physical emotions. Blue, of the right tint, will tend to cause feelings of spirituality, religious emotion, etc. Green is conducive to feelings of relaxation, repose, quiet, etc. Black produces the feeling of gloom and grief. And so on, each color tends to produce emotional vibrations similar to those which manifest that particular color in the astral aura of the person. It is a case of "give and take" along the entire scale of color and emotions, according to the great natural laws.

While the explanation of these facts is not known to the average person, nevertheless nearly everyone recognizes the subtle effect of color and avoids certain colors, while seeking certain others. There is not a single living human being but who has experienced the sense of rest, calm, repose, and calm inflow of strength, when in a room decorated in quiet shades of green. Nature, herself, has given this particular shade to the grass and leaves of trees and plants, so that the soothing effect of the country scene is produced. The aura of a person experiencing these feelings, and yielding to them, will manifest precisely the tint or shade of green which is shown on the grass and leaves around him, so true is this natural law of action and reaction.

The effect of scarlet upon animals, the bull for instance, is well known—to use the familiar term, it causes one to "see red." The sight of the color of blood is apt to arouse feelings of rage, or disgust, by reason of the same law. The sight of the beautiful clear blue sky tends to arouse feelings of reverence, awe or spirituality. One can never think of this shade of blue arousing rage; or red arouse feelings of spirituality.

It is a well known fact that in insane asylums, the use of red in decorations must be avoided, while the proper shades of blue or green are favored. On the other hand, the use of a proper red, in certain cases, will tend to arouse vitality and physical strength in a patient. It is not by mere chance that the life giving blood is a bright, rich red color when it leaves the heart.

When one "feels blue" he does not have the impression of a bright or soft blue—but he really is almost conscious of the presence of a dull bluish gray. And the presence of such a color in one's surroundings, tends to cause a feeling of depression. Everyone knows the effect of a "gray day" in the Fall or Spring.

Again, who does not know the feeling of mental exaltation coming from the sight of a day filled with golden sunshine, or from a golden sunset. We find proofs of this law of Nature on all sides, every day of our lives. It is an interesting subject, which will repay the student for the expenditure of a little time and thought upon it.

Speaking of the general class characteristics of the three primary groups of colors, all occultists, as well as many physiologists and psychologists, are agreed on the following fundamental propositions, viz.: that (1) Red is exciting to the mind and emotions; (2) Yellow is inspiring and elevating, and intellectually stimulating; and (3) Blue is cool, soothing, and calming. It is also universally conceded that the right shades of green (combining the qualities of blue and yellow in appropriate proportions) is the ideal color of rest and recuperation, followed by a stimulation and new ambition. The reason for this may be seen, when you consider the respective qualities of blue and yellow which compose this color.

It is interesting to note that the science of medicine is now seriously considering the use of colors in the treatment of disease, and the best medical authorities investigating the subject are verifying the teachings of the old occultists, regarding the influence of colors on mental states and physical conditions.

Dr. Edwin Babbitt, a pioneer in this line in the Western world, gave the general principles in a nutshell, when he laid down the following rule: "There is a trianal series of graduations in the peculiar potencies of colors, the center and climax of electrical action, which cools the nerves, being in violet; the climax of electrical action, which is soothing to the vascular system, being in blue; the climax of luminosity being in yellow; and the climax of thermism or heat being in red. This is not an imaginary division of qualities, but a real one, the flamelike red color having a principle of warmth in itself; the blue and violet, a principle of cold and electricity. Thus we have many styles of chromatic action, including progression of hues, of lights and shades, of fineness and coarseness, of electrical power, luminous power, thermal power, etc."

Read the above statement of Dr. Babbitt, and then compare it with the occult teaching regarding the astral colors, and you will perceive the real basis of the science which the good doctor sought to establish, and in which cause he did such excellent pioneer work. The result of his work is now being elaborated by modern physicians in the great schools of medicine, particularly on the Continent, in Europe—England and America being somewhat behind the times in this work.

The advanced occultist also finds much satisfaction in the interest, on the part of physicians and jurists, in the matter of the influence of color upon the mental, moral and physical welfare of the public. The effect of color upon morality is being noticed by workers for human welfare, occupying important offices.

The American journals report the case of a judge in a large Western city in that country, who insisted upon his courtroom being decorated in light, cheerful tints, instead of in the old, gloomy, depressing shades formerly employed. This judge wisely remarked that brightness led to right thinking, and darkness to crooked thinking; also that his court, being an uplift court, must have walls to correspond, and that it was enough to turn any man into a criminal to be compelled to sit in a dark, dismal courtroom, day after day.

This good judge, who must have had some acquaintance with the occult teachings, is quoted as concluding as follows: "White, cream, light yellow, and orange are the colors which are the sanest. I might add light green, for that is the predominant color in Nature; black, brown and deep red are incentives to crime—a man in anger sees red." Surely a remarkable utterance from the bench!

The effect of color schemes upon the moral and mental welfare of persons is being recognized in the direction of providing brighter color schemes in schools, hospitals, reformatories, prisons, etc. The reports naturally show the correctness of the underlying theory. The color of a tiny flower has its effect upon even the most hardened prisoner; while the minds of children in school are quickened by a touch of brightness here and there in the room. It needs no argument to prove the beneficial effect of the right kind of colors in the sickroom, or hospital ward.

The prevailing theories, and practice, regarding the employment of color in therapeutics and human welfare work, are in the main correct. But, I urge the study of the occult significance of color, as mentioned in this book in connection with the human aura and its astral colors, as a sound basis for an intelligent, thorough understanding of the real psychic principles underlying the physical application of the methods referred to. Go to the center of the subject, and then work outward—that is the true rule of the occultist, which might well be followed by the non-occult general public.

CHAPTER VIII
AURIC MAGNETISM

The phenomenon of human magnetism is too well recognized by the general public, to require argument at this time. Let the scientists dispute about it as much as they please, down in the heart of nearly all of the plain people of the race is the conviction that there is such a thing. The occultists, of course, are quite familiar with the wonderful manifestations of this great natural force, and with its effect upon the minds and bodies of members of the race, and can afford to smile at the attempts of some of the narrow minds in the colleges to pooh-pooh the matter.

But the average person is not familiar with the relation of this human magnetism to the human aura. I think that the student should familiarize himself with this fundamental relation, in order to reason correctly on the subject of human magnetism. Here is the fundamental fact in a nutshell: The human aura is the great storehouse, or reservoir, of human magnetism, and is the source of all human magnetism that is projected by the individual toward other individuals. Just how human magnetism is generated, is, of course, a far deeper matter, but it is enough for our purpose at this time to explain the fact of its storage and transmission.

In cases of magnetic healing, etc., the matter is comparatively simple. In such instances the healer by an effort of the will (sometimes unconsciously applied) projects a supply of his pranic aura vibrations into the body of his patient, by way of the nervous system of the patient, and also by means of what may be called the induction of the aura itself.

The mere presence of a person strongly charged with prana, is often enough to cause an overflow into the aura of other persons, with a resulting feeling of new strength and energy. By the use of the hands of the healer, a heightened effect is produced, by reason of certain properties inherent in the nervous system of both healer and patient.

There is even a flow of etheric substance from the aura of the healer to that of the patient, in cases where the vitality of the latter is very low. Many a healer has actually, and literally, pumped his life force and etheric substance into the body of his patient, when the latter was sinking into the weakness which precedes death, and has by so doing been able to bring him back to life and strength. This is practically akin to the transfusion of blood—except that it is on the psychic plane instead of the physical.

But the work of the magnetic healer does not stop here, if he be well informed regarding his science. The educated healer realizing the potent effect of mental states upon physical conditions—of mental vibrations upon the physical nerve centers and organs of the body—endeavors to arouse the proper mental vibrations in the mind of his patient. Ordinarily, he does this merely by holding in his mind the corresponding desired mental state, and thus arousing similar vibrations in the mind of the patient. This of itself is a powerful weapon of healing, and constitutes the essence of mental healing as usually practiced. But there is a possible improvement even upon this, as we shall see in a moment.

The advanced occultist, realizing the law of action and reaction in the matter of the auric colors, turns the same to account in healing work, as follows: He not only holds in his mind the strong feeling and thought which he wishes to transmit to the patient, but (fix this in your mind) he also pictures in his imagination the particular kind of color which corresponds with the feeling or thought in question.

A moment's thought will show you that by this course he practically multiplies the effect. Not only do his own thought vibrations (1) set up corresponding vibrations in the mind of the patient, by the laws of thought transference, but (2) his thought of the certain colors will set up corresponding vibrations not only (a) in his own aura, and thence (b) to that of the patient, but will also (3) act directly upon the aura of the patient and reproduce the colors there, which (4) in turn will arouse corresponding vibrations in the mind of the patient, by the law of reaction.

The above may sound a little complicated at first reading, but a little analysis will show you that it is really quite a simple process, acting strictly along the lines of Action and Reaction, which law has been explained to you in preceding chapters of this book. The vibrations rebound from mind to aura, and from aura to mind, in the patient, something like a billiard ball flying from one side of the table to another, or a tennis ball flying between the two racquets over the net.

The principle herein mentioned may be employed as well in what is called "absent treatment" as in treatments where the patient is present. By the laws of thought transference, not only the thought but also the mental image of the appropriate astral color, is transmitted over space, and then, impinging on the mind of the patient, is transmitted into helpful and health-giving vibrations in his mind. The healer of any school of mental or spiritual healing will find this plan very helpful to him in giving absent as well as present treatments. I recommend it from years of personal experience, as well as that of other advanced occultists.

Of course the fact that the ordinary healer is not able to distinguish the finer shades of astral color, by reason of his not having actually perceived them manifested in the aura, renders his employment of this method less efficacious than that of the developed and trained occultist. But, nevertheless, he will find that, from the knowledge of the auric or astral colors given in this little book, he will be able to obtain quite satisfactory and marked results in his practice. The following table, committed to memory, will be of help to him in the matter of employing the mental image of the auric colors in his healing work.

TABLE OF HEALING COLORS.

Nervous System—

>Cooling and soothing: Shades of violet, lavender, etc.
>Resting and invigorating effect: Grass greens.
>Inspiring and illuminating: Medium yellows, and orange.
>Stimulating and exciting: Reds (bright).

Blood and Organs—

>Cooling and soothing: Clear dark blues.
>Resting and invigorating: Grass greens.
>Inspiring and illuminating: Orange yellows.
>Stimulating and exciting: Bright reds.

The following additional suggestions will be found helpful to the healer: In cases of impaired physical vitality; also chilliness, lack of bodily warmth, etc., bright, warm reds are indicated. In cases of feverishness, overheated blood, excessive blood pressure, inflammation, etc., blue is indicated. Red has a tendency to produce renewed and more active heart action; while violets and lavenders tend to slow down the too rapid beating of the heart. A nervous, unstrung patient, may be treated by bathing her, mentally, in a flood of violet or lavender auric color; while a tired, used up, fatigued person may be invigorated by flooding him with bright reds, followed by bright, rich yellows, finishing the treatment with a steady flow of warm orange color.

To those who are sufficiently advanced in occult philosophy, I would say that they should remember the significance of the Great White Light, and accordingly conclude their treatment by an effort to indicate an approach to that clear, pure white color in the aura—mentally, of course. This will leave the patient in an inspired, exalted, illuminated state of mind and soul, which will be of great benefit to him, and will also have the effect of reinvigorating the healer by cosmic energy or para-prana.

Everything that has been said in this chapter regarding the use of color in magnetic treatments, is equally applicable to cases of self-healing, or self-treatment. Let the patient follow the directions above given for the healer, and then turn the healing current, or thought, inward—and the result will be the same as if he were treating another. The individual will soon find that certain colors fit his requirements better than others, in which case let him follow such experience in preference to general rules, for the intuition generally is the safest guide in such cases. However, it will be found that the individual experience will usually agree with the tables given above, with slight personal variations.

CHAPTER IX

DEVELOPING THE AURA

When it is remembered that the aura of the individual affects and influences other persons with whom he comes in contact—and is, in fact, an important part of his personality—it will be seen that it is important that the individual take pains to develop his aura in the direction of desirable qualities, and to neutralize and weed out undesirable ones. This becomes doubly true when it is also remembered that, according to the law of action and reaction, the auric vibrations react upon the mind of the individual, thus intensifying and adding fuel to the original mental states which called them forth. From any point of view, it is seen to be an important part of self development and character building, to develop the aura according to scientific occult principles.

In this work of aura development, there is found to be two correlated phases, namely: (1) the direct work of flooding the aura with the best vibrations, by means of holding in the mind clear, distinct and repeated mental pictures of desirable ideas and feelings; and (2) the added effect of mental images of the colors corresponding to the ideas and feelings which are deemed desirable and worthy of development.

The first of the above mentioned phases is probably far more familiar to the average student, than is the second. This from the fact that the average student is apt to be more or less familiar with the teachings of the numerous schools or cults which agree in the axiom that "holding the thought" tends to develop the mind of the individual along the particular lines of such thought.

This is a correct psychological principle, for that matter, even when those practicing it do not fully understand the underlying facts. Mental faculties, like physical muscles, tend to develop by exercise and use, and any faculty may be developed and cultivated in this way.

Another teaching of these same schools is that the character of the thoughts so "held" by the individual, effects other persons with whom he comes in contact, and, in a way attracts to him objective things, persons, and circumstances in harmony with such thoughts. This also is in accordance with the best occult teaching—from which, of course, it was originally derived.

I heartily endorse the facts of these teachings, and pronounce them fundamentally correct. And, in this connection, I may say that every healer may apply his own methods PLUS this teaching regarding the aura, and thus obtain greatly increased results.

By the faithful, persevering, holding in mind of certain ideas and feelings, the individual may flood his aura with the vibrations and colors of such ideas and feelings, and thus charge it with auric energy and power. By so doing, he gains the benefit of the reaction upon his own mind, and also secures the advantage of the effect thereof upon other persons with whom he comes in contact. In this way he not only builds up his individual character along desirable lines, but at the same time develops a strong, positive, attractive "personality" which affects others with whom he comes in contact.

I do not consider it necessary to go into details here regarding this phase of "holding the thought," for, as I have said, the average student is already familiar with the rules regarding the same. In a nutshell, however, I will say that each individual is largely the result of the thoughts he has manifested, and the feelings which he has harbored. Therefore, the rule is to manifest and exercise the faculties you would develop, and inhibit or refrain from manifesting the ones you would restrain or control. Again, to restrain an undesirable faculty, develop and exercise its opposite—kill out the negatives by developing the positives. The mind produces thought; and yet, it tends to grow from the particular portion of its own product which you may choose to feed to it—for it not only creates thought, but also feeds upon it. So, finally, let it produce the best kind of thought for you, and then throw that back into the hopper, for it will use it to grind out more of the same kind and grow strong in so doing. That is the whole thing in a nutshell.

The second phase of aura development (as above classified), however, is not likely to be familiar to the average student, for the reason that it is not known outside of advanced occult circles, and very little has been allowed to be taught regarding it. But, the very reticence regarding it is a proof of its importance, and I strongly advise my students to give to it the attention and practice that its importance merits. The practice, thereof, however, is extremely simple, and the principle of the practice, moreover, is based solely upon the facts of the relation of color and mental states, as shown in the astral auric colors, as fully explained in the preceding chapters of this book.

In order to intelligently practice the development of the aura by means of flooding or charging it with the vibrations of psychic colors, it is first necessary that the student be thoroughly familiar with the scale of colors related to each set of mental states or emotional feelings. This scale and its key is found in a number of places in the preceding chapters.

The student should turn back the pages of this book, and then carefully re-read and re-study every word which has been said about the relation of mental states and auric colors. He should know the mental correspondence of the shades of red, yellow, and blue, so thoroughly that the thought of one will bring the idea of the other. He should be able to think of the corresponding group of colors, the moment he thinks of any particular mental state. He should be thoroughly familiar with the physical, mental, and spiritual effect of any of the colors, and should moreover, test himself, psychically, for the individual effects of certain colors upon himself.

He should enter into this study with interest and earnestness, and then by keeping his eyes and ears open, he will perceive interesting facts concerning the subject on every side in his daily work and life. He will perceive many proofs of the principle, and will soon amass a stock of experiences illustrating each color and its corresponding mental state. He will be richly repaid for the work of such study, which, in fact, will soon grow to be more like pleasure than like work.

Having mastered this phase of the subject, the student should give himself a thorough, honest, self-examination and mental analysis. He should write down a chart of his strong points and his weak ones. He should check off the traits which should be developed, and those which should be restrained. He should determine whether he needs development along physical, mental, and spiritual lines, and in what degree. Having made this chart of himself, he should then apply the principles of charging the aura with the color vibrations indicated by his self diagnosis and prescription.

The last stage is quite simple, once one has acquired the general idea back of it. It consists simply in forming as clear a mental image as possible of the color or colors desired, and then projecting the vibrations into the aura by the simple effort of the will. This does not mean that one needs to clinch the fist or frown the brow, in willing. Willing, in the occult sense, may be said to consist of a **COMMAND**, leaving the rest to the mechanism of the will and mind. Take away the obstacle of Doubt and Fear—then the Royal Command performs the work of setting the will into operation. This, by the way, is an important occult secret, of wide application—try to master its all important significance.

The mental imaging of colors may be materially aided by concentration upon physical material of the right color. By concentrating the attention and vision upon a red flower, for instance; or upon a bit of green leaf, in another instance; one may be able to form a clear, positive mental image of that particular color. This accompanied by the willing, and demand, that the vibrations of this color shall charge the aura, will be found to accomplish the result. Have something around you showing the desirable colors, and your attention will almost instinctively take up the impression thereof, even though you may be thinking of, or doing something else. Live as much as possible in the idea and presence of the desirable color, and you will get the habit of setting up the mental image and vibration thereof. A little practice and experience will soon give you the idea, and enable you to get the best results. Patience, perseverance, and sustained earnest interest—that is the key of success.

CHAPTER X

THE PROTECTIVE AURA

Among the very oldest of the teachings of occultism, we find instructions regarding the building up and maintenance of the protective aura of the individual, whereby he renders himself immune to undesirable physical, mental, psychic or spiritual influences. So important is this teaching, that it is to be regretted that there has not been more said on the subject by some of the writers of recent years. The trouble with many of these recent writers is that they seem to wish to close their eyes to the unpleasant facts of life, and to gaze only upon the pleasant ones. But this is a mistake, for ignorance has never been a virtue, and to shut one's eyes to unpleasant facts does not always result in destroying them. I consider any teaching unfinished and inadequate which does not include instruction along protective lines.

Physical auric protection consists in charging the aura with vital magnetism and color, which will tend to ward off not only the physical contagion of ill persons, but, what is often still more important, the contagion of their mind and feelings.

The student who has really studied the preceding chapters will at once realize that this protection is afforded by filling the aura with the vibrations of health and physical strength, by means of the mental imaging of the life-preserving reds, and the exercise of the mind in the direction of thought of strength and power. These two things will tend to greatly increase the resistive aura of anyone, and enable him to throw off disease influences which affect others.

The aura of the successful physician and healer, in the presence of disease, will invariably show the presence of the bright, positive red in the aura, accompanied by the mental vibrations of strength, power and confidence, and the absence of fear. This in connection with the Auric Circle, which shall be described presently, will be of great value to healers, physicians, nurses, etc., as well as to those who are brought into intimate contact with sick persons.

Of practically the same degree of importance, is the charging of the aura with the vibrations of mental protection, viz, the vibrations of orange, yellow and similar colors. These are the colors of intellect, you will remember, and when the aura is charged and flooded with them it acts as a protection against the efforts of others to convince one against his will, by sophistical arguments, plausible reasoning, fallacious illustrations, etc. It gives to one a sort of mental illumination, quickening the perceptive faculties, and brightening up the reasoning and judging powers, and finally, giving a sharp edge to the powers of repartee and answer.

If you will assume the right positive mental attitude, and will flood your aura with the vibrations of the mental orange-yellow, the mental efforts of other persons will rebound from your aura, or, to use another figure of speech, will slip from it like water from the back of the proverbial duck. It is well to carry the mental image of your head being surrounded by a golden aura or halo, at such times—this will be found especially efficacious as a protective helmet when you are assaulted by the intellect or arguments of others.

And, again, there is a third form of protective aura, namely protection of one's emotional nature—and this is highly important, when one remembers how frequently we are moved to action by our emotions, rather than by our intellect or reason. To guard one's emotions, is to guard one's very inmost soul, so to speak. If we can protect our feeling and emotional side, we will be able to use our reasoning powers and intellect far more effectively, as all know by experience.

What color should we use in this form of auric protection? Can anyone be in doubt here, if he has read the preceding chapters? What is the emotional protective color?—why, blue, of course. Blue controls this part of the mind or soul, and by raising ourselves into the vibrations of positive blue, we leave behind us the lower emotions and feelings, and are transported into the higher realms of the soul where these low vibrations and influences cannot follow us. In the same way, the blue colored aura will act as an armor to protect us from the contagion of the low passions and feelings of others.

If you are subjected to evil influences, or contagion of those harboring low emotions and desires, you will do well to acquire the art of flooding your aura with the positive blue tints. Make a study of bright, clear blues, and you will instinctively select the one best suited for your needs. Nature gives us this instinctive knowledge, if we will but seek for it, and then apply it when found. The aura of great moral teachers, great priests and preachers, advanced occultists, in fact all men of lofty ideals working among those lower on the moral scale, are always found to be charged with a beautiful, clear blue, which acts as a protection to them when they are unduly exposed to moral or emotional contagion. Ignorance of the occult laws have caused the downfall of many a great moral teacher, who could have protected himself in this way, in times of strong attack of low vibrations, had he but known the truth. The individual who knows this law, and who applies it, is rendered absolutely immune from evil contagion on the emotional plane of being.

THE GREAT AURIC CIRCLE.

But no occult instruction on this subject would be complete without a reference to the Great Auric Circle of Protection, which is a shelter to the soul, mind, and body, against outside psychic influences, directed, consciously or unconsciously against the individual. In these days of wide spread though imperfect, knowledge of psychic phenomena, it is especially important that one should be informed as to this great shield of protection. Omitting all reference to the philosophy underlying it, it may be said that this Auric Circle is formed by making the mental image, accompanied by the demand of will, of the aura being surrounded by a great band of PURE CLEAR WHITE LIGHT. A little perseverance will enable you to create this on the astral plane, and, though (unless you have the astral vision) you cannot see it actually, yet you will actually FEEL its protective presence, so that you will know that it is there guarding you.

This White Auric Circle will be an effective and infallible armor against all forms of psychic attack or influence, no matter from whom it may emanate, or whether directed consciously or unconsciously. It is a perfect and absolute protection, and the knowledge of its protective power should be sufficient to drive fear from the heart of all who have dreaded psychic influence, "malicious animal magnetism" (so-called), or anything else of the kind, by whatever name known. It is also a protection against psychic vampirism, or draining of magnetic strength.

The Auric Circle is, of course, really egg-shaped, or oval, for it fringes the aura as the shell cases the egg. See yourself, mentally, as surrounded by this Great White Auric Circle of Protection, and let the idea sink into your consciousness. Realize its power over the influences from outside, and rejoice in the immunity it gives you.

The Auric Circle, however, will admit any outside impressions that you really desire to come to you, while shutting out the others. That is, with this exception, that if your inner soul recognizes that some of these desired influences and impressions are apt to harm you (though your reason and feeling know it not) then will such impressions be denied admittance. For the White Light is the radiation of Spirit, which is higher than ordinary mind, emotion, or body and is Master of All. And its power, even though we can but imperfectly represent it even mentally, is such that before its energy, and in its presence, in the aura, all lower vibrations are neutralized and disintegrated.

The highest and deepest occult teaching is that the White Light must never be used for purpose of attack or personal gain, but that it may properly be used by anyone, at any time, to protect against outside psychic influences against which the soul protests. It is the armor of the soul, and may well be employed whenever or wherever the need arises.

Throughout the pages of this little book have been scattered crumbs of teaching other than those concerning the aura alone. Those for whom these are intended will recognize and appropriate them—the others will not see them, and will pass them by. One attracts his own to him. Much seed must fall on waste places, in order that here and there a grain will find lodgment in rich soil awaiting its coming. True occult knowledge is practical power and strength. Beware of prostituting the higher teachings for selfish ends and ignoble purposes. To guard and preserve your own will is right; to seek to impose your will upon that of another is wrong. Passive resistance is often the strongest form of resistance—this is quite different from non-resistance.

www.ingramcontent.com/pod-product-compliance
Lightning Source LLC
Chambersburg PA
CBHW021116020426
42331CB00004B/519